What if we do

NOTHING?

RAIN FOREST DESTRUCTION

Ewan McLeish

**Consultant: Rob Bowden, Specialist in
Global Environmental and Social Issues**

WORLD ALMANAC® LIBRARY

Please visit our web site at: www.garethstevens.com
For a free color catalog describing World Almanac® Library's list of
high-quality books and multimedia programs, call 1-800-848-2928 (USA)
or 1-800-387-3178 (Canada). World Almanac® Library's fax: (414) 332-3567.

Library of Congress Cataloging-in-Publication Data

McLeish, Ewan, 1950-
    Rain forest destruction / Ewan McLeish.
        p. cm. – (What if we do nothing?)
    Includes bibliographical references and index.
    ISBN-13: 978-0-8368-7758-8 (lib. bdg.)
    ISBN-13: 978-0-8368-8158-5 (softcover)
    1. Rain forest ecology–Juvenile literature. 2. Rain forest conservation–Juvenile literature.
3. Rain forests–Juvenile literature. 4. Deforestation–Tropics–Juvenile literature. I. Title.
QH541.5.R27M40   2007
578.734–dc22   2006030448

First published in 2007 by
World Almanac® Library
A Member of the WRC Media Family of Companies
330 West Olive Street, Suite 100
Milwaukee, WI 53212 USA

Produced by Arcturus Publishing Limited
Editor: Alex Woolf
Designer: Peta Morey
Picture researcher: Glass Onion Pictures

World Almanac® Library editorial direction: Valerie J. Weber
World Almanac® Library editor: Leifa Butrick
World Almanac® Library art direction: Tammy West
World Almanac® Library graphic design: Charlie Dahl
World Almanac® Library production: Jessica Yanke and Robert Kraus

Picture credits: CORBIS: 5 (RICKEY ROGERS/Reuters/CORBIS), 6 (Vic Kintanar/epa/CORBIS),
9 (Tony Arruza/CORBIS), 10 (Zainal Abd Halim/Reuters/CORBIS), 12 (Joel Creed; Eye
Ubiquitous/CORBIS), 15 and cover (Kazuyoshi Nomachi/CORBIS), 16 and cover (Karen
Kasmauski/CORBIS), 19 (Joe McDonald/CORBIS), 20 (Renee Lynn/CORBIS),
25 (Reuters/CORBIS), 29 (Reuters/CORBIS), 30 (Colin MacPherson/Colin McPherson/CORBIS),
33 (Janet Jarman/CORBIS), 35 (Bob Krist/CORBIS), 37 (Reuters/CORBIS),
38 (David A. Northcott/CORBIS), 41 (Wolfgang Kaehler/CORBIS), 42 (Dan Lamont/CORBIS).
Rex Features: 22 (Lehtikuva OY/Rex Features), 26 and cover (Paul Raffaele/Rex Features),
44 (Patrick Frillet/Rex Features).

Printed in China

1 2 3 4 5 6 7 8 9 10 09 08 07 06

Contents

CHAPTER 1

Paradise Lost

It is 2045, and most of the world's tropical rain forests have disappeared. Those that remain are either protected in nature reserves or are now too small to support the huge range of animals and plants that once lived in them. Much of the land that was once rain forest has turned to desert. The soil that was protected by the roots of the giant forest trees for millions of years has been washed away. The farms that replaced the forests are gone, too. Landslides engulfed whole towns and villages, and great seas of mud slid and slithered down the treeless mountains and hillsides.

More than 50 percent of all animal and plant species that live on land may be extinct by the year 2045. Many of the indigenous (native) people may have left the forest as the result of disease or simply because they could no longer sustain their rain-forest way of life. As the land deteriorated, poor farmers may have flocked to the cities to find jobs. There would not be enough jobs for everyone, so the farmers' anxiety led to rioting over high unemployment.

How Could Such Destruction Take Place?

Such destruction is possible if groups of people continue to clear the rain forests to get timber and minerals and to create farmland, carving huge roads across the rain forests and leaving them exposed to further exploitation. If people fail to replace the cleared trees, much of the stripped earth will never recover.

The Consequences

These possible consequences are serious and frightening. Rain forests cover about 2.3 million square miles (6 million square kilometers)—an area a little more than three times the size of Texas. Although some rain forests are so remote that they probably will not be cleared, currently rain forests are being destroyed at a rate of about 80,000 acres (32,000 hectares) per day, or nearly 30 million acres (12 million ha) or 46,300 square miles (120,000 sq km) per year. If you divide the area of rain forest that is left—2.3 million square miles (6 million sq km)—by the annual rate in square miles (kilometers) at which they are being destroyed—460,000 square miles (120,000 sq km)—you get the number of years left before almost all rain forest is gone if we do nothing—50 years.

Types of Forest

Tropical rain forests (the type this book deals with) receive large amounts of rainfall all year round. They extend from the equator to the tropics. Boreal temperate rain forests are cooler and found north and south of the two tropics in countries such as Canada, the United States, and Russia. Not surprisingly, tropical rain forests are much warmer than temperate rain forests and contain the greatest diversity of life of any land habitat. Primary rain forest is original, natural forest; secondary rain forest is where replanting has occurred.

This rain forest in the Amazon Basin has been cleared by loggers. In forty or fifty years' time, if we continue to destroy rain forests at the current rate, this bare land could be all that is left of most of them.

OVERALL RATES OF TROPICAL DEFORESTATION*

| | Total Forest Cover (2005) | | Total Deforestation |
	Million Acres (Ha)	% Total Land Area	% Loss since 1990
Central America	55.4 (22.4)	43.9	-18.9
South America	2,050 (832)	47.7	-6.7
Southeast Asia	700 (283)	33.4	-12.4
Australia and Pacific Islands (Oceania)	510 (206)	24.3	-2.9
Africa	1,380 (559)	34.3	-9.9

*Note: These figures are for the regions as a whole; some deforested areas were covered with other types of forest, although the majority was rain forest land.

Source: mongabay/FAO/CFAN

Mountains on the Move

On February 17, 2006, a mud slide swept down the mountainsides above the farming village of Guinsaugon in the Philippines. Villagers were buried beneath the thick, gooey mud, and eighteen hundred were killed. The mud slide also swept away an entire school. Prolonged rains and unstable soil were among the many reasons given for the disaster. Many blamed the clearing of forests high above the buried village because, with nothing to hold the soil in place, nothing could hold the mountain in place either.

Rescue workers confront scenes of total devastation after a landslide engulfed a village in the Philippines in 2005. Images like this may become increasingly common as forest cover on hillsides is removed, allowing landslides to destroy towns and villages.

A Freak Event?

Sadly, the Guinsaugon mud slide was not an isolated event. Many other villages on the islands that make up Indonesia in Southeast Asia are repeatedly devastated by landslides. Some of the most aggressive logging policies in the world affect Indonesia, where whole areas of forest are stripped of trees.

We need to understand why rain-forest destruction happens. We need to understand that individuals' or industries' carelessness or greed are not the only causes for the loss of the rain forests. The poverty and desperation of the people involved also figure in, and no simple solutions are readily available.

Can we stop rain-forest destruction now? Further loss is inevitable, even if decisive action were taken today. Our best hope is to reduce the rate at which the destruction takes place and then gradually turn the situation around. It is not solely the responsibility of others or of governments on the other side of the world: we all have a role to play. We may not want our children, or their children, to ask, "Why did you do nothing?"

WHAT WOULD YOU DO?

You are concerned that most of the world's rain forests may disappear in your lifetime. You want your school to run a one-day program on the future of rain forests. How do you convince your teachers that this would be a worthwhile idea?

- You argue that discussing real issues that affect your future and that of others is a key aspect of your education.

- You argue that there will not be much of a future if we ignore issues like the destruction of rain forests.

See the discussion on page 47 for suggestions.

CHAPTER 2

Rain Forests in Retreat

It is 2020, and rain forests are now being attacked on all sides. A number of world organizations are meeting to discuss the state of the world's rain forests as an urgent priority. The United Nations Environment Program (UNEP) is hosting this meeting, but other organizations involved include the World Resources Institute and the Food and Agriculture Organization (FAO) as well as the World Bank. Some delegates have protested the presence of the World Bank at this meeting because they believe that the bank's policies support large-scale development projects, such as dam and road construction, that allow poor countries to build up huge debts. They criticize the World Bank's representatives for having contributed to the problem they are there to discuss. Others think it is too late for blame. As one senior delegate puts it, "We all have to work together now; if we don't get it right this time, we will not get another chance."

Getting behind the Headlines

Before looking at the real causes of rain-forest destruction, it is important to understand some of the factors that create situations in which deforestation can occur. In 2000, the population of the world was 6 billion; by 2013, it is estimated that it will be 7 billion, and by 2028, 8 billion. Much of this growth will occur in poor or rapidly developing countries—such as those in parts of South America, Africa, and Asia—that are least able to deal with the increase. Many of these people are, or will be, living in extreme poverty. Poverty is not a cause of deforestation, but it creates a situation in which people are forced to take desperate measures to survive. For example, they may even destroy their own environments by farming rain-forest land in ways that cause permanent damage to the soil.

Debt is also a factor. Many poor or developing countries owe large amounts of money to banks and other agencies in the richer countries. Most find it hard just to keep up with interest payments.

Some of these debts are in the process of being written off, but the basic problem remains. Like poor people, poor countries are forced to take short-term measures, like exploiting their forests for timber when, in the long run, they would be more valuable left standing.

Low-income people in Honduras have neither the time nor the resources to look after their land. Soon this land will be useless, and the family will move on to clear more forest.

RUNNING TO STAND STILL

Brazil is undergoing an export boom, but its desire to export is driven by its need to pay back its massive foreign debt. Three-quarters of its foreign earnings go to paying off its debt of about $250 billion. Debt service has put pressure on the country to increase international exports, such as timber, beef, and soybeans. More rain forests, therefore, are cleared to make such income-earning activities easier.

A Family Matter

Perhaps surprisingly, the single biggest cause of deforestation is the family farm. In the past, farming families living on or near the edges of forests would clear the forest margins to plant and grow crops, mainly to feed themselves. They used methods that were in harmony with the land's ability to recover. They planted crops to support the farming family, such as corn, beans, cassavas, and plantains. They allowed long fallow periods during which they did not grow crops. This method allowed the soil to regenerate. In the meantime, the family would move, or shift, to cultivate a new plot nearby.

This so-called shifting cultivation did not generally harm the rain forests. In fact, it was sometimes even beneficial because the margins between the forest and the cultivated land provided a slightly different kind of environment that attracted a range of wild animals and plants. Problems arose, however, when poverty forced more and more people to set up farms at the forest edges. Often

A plantation worker tends oil palm fruits. These yield valuable palm oil that is exported worldwide and used to make margarine, cooking oils, and cookies. In Indonesia, palm oil makes up nearly 80 percent of all exports. Although plantations are often located on land already cleared of rain forest, they can still create problems such as pollution of water supplies and loss of wildlife.

they lacked the skills of the traditional shifting cultivators, so the farms failed. The pressure caused by the increasing population even forced the traditional farmers to reduce the fallow period because there was less and less land available to farm.

Thus, the traditional systems of farming became less sustainable. The old way of shifting cultivation, which had been successful for perhaps thousands of years, became destructive. The forest edges were cleared by cutting and burning because the ash added valuable plant nutrients to the soil. Crops were planted—traditional varieties, as well as so-called cash crops, such as coffee and citrus fruits—to sell to local buyers. With no time allowed for regeneration, the soil was exhausted within a few years, and the farmland had to be abandoned. Meanwhile, the family—and hundreds of thousands like them—moved on to clear new forest. It is estimated that these unsustainable farming methods now account for nearly two-thirds of all deforestation. It may seem strange that this way of life can have such a devastating effect on the great rain forests, but a single family may clear enormous areas over a period of time. Also, rain-forest soils themselves are already quite thin and poor in nutrients, and they are quickly depleted.

COUNTRIES WITH HIGHEST ANNUAL DEFORESTATION RATE, 2000-2005 [SQUARE MILES (SQ KM)]	
Brazil	13,390 (34,660)
Indonesia	5,590 (14,478)
Mexico	1525 (3,950)
Papua New Guinea	966 (2,502)
Peru	867(2,246)
Bolivia	522 (1,352)
Sudan	455 (1,178)
Nigeria	317 (820)
Cambodia	266 (668)
Colombia	216 (561)

Source: FAO/Mongabay

Plantation Damage

The much bigger agricultural businesses grow commercial crops, including palm oil, rubber, soybeans, coffee, cacao, and tropical fruits, on huge tracts of land. They have a double effect: first, they occupy the best, most fertile soils, usually located in valleys. As a result, rural populations have to move onto less fertile soil or are forced to clear new forest to survive. Second, they clear forested land themselves, often paying for the project with government funds. This type of commercial agriculture may also bring further problems, such as contamination of soil with pesticides and damage to the health of farm laborers who use them. In addition, many of these crops require much greater amounts of water than indigenous (local) varieties, resulting in too much water being taken from the ground.

Meanwhile, Back at the Ranch . . .

Cattle ranching, especially in Central and South America, is another major cause of deforestation. In the past, ranchers preferred the more easily managed rangelands of dry forest and savannah farther from the equator. Later, they turned their attention to the moist tropical rain forests. Ranchers operate in two main ways. First, they may occupy large tracts of forest and clear the land themselves. Alternatively, they buy up land that has already been cleared by farmers and convert this into pasture. Once the land is converted and fenced, the rancher may sublease the land to other farmers and then move deeper into the forest to repeat the cycle.

Since the 1950s, the land area under permanent pasture for ranching has increased from 9.6 million acres (3.9 million ha) to 33 million acres (13.4 million ha) in Central America alone. Much of this increase has come at the expense of the region's tropical rain forest. Ranching is an attractive alternative to other land uses because it is reasonably profitable in the short run, requires little labor, and has huge markets, such as the United States and Europe. As people in the richer countries have become more aware

Cattle ranching for the beef market in Central and South America is profitable, but cleared forest soils are fragile and easily damaged by trampling. In the past, beef production was important to export to the United States, Europe, and Japan. More recently, however, cattle are being reared for the rapidly growing domestic (home) market, increasing the pressure to clear more land.

GOING UP IN SMOKE

Forest fires destroy or damage between 14.8 and 34.6 million acres (6 and 14 million ha) of tropical forest every year. That figure is about equal to the damage caused by logging and conversion to agriculture combined! Often the fires are started deliberately as a way of illegally clearing more forest. Severe fires in Indonesia in 1997 caused high levels of air pollution, affecting 75 million people overall. Fires have a double impact: they add significantly to carbon dioxide (CO_2) in the atmosphere, and the destruction of the trees removes the rain forests' ability to absorb the polluting gases.

of the damaging effects of their demand for cheap imported beef, some of this demand has decreased. As some of the countries with rain forests become wealthier, however, their people's greater demand for beef keeps the beef market high at the expense of their forests. In addition, the demand to grow soybeans for cattle feed is increasing, resulting in the expansion of plantations.

Clearing Forests for Fuel

For most of the world's poor, wood is the only source of fuel available to them. In fact, 80 percent of all wood used worldwide is for fuel. Many people who use wood as a source of energy are the rural poor, and they gather mostly naturally fallen dead wood. Wood, which has often been converted into charcoal first, is also a major fuel in the cities. Collecting wood for fuel does not necessarily destroy rain forests, but it does damage or degrade them. Sometimes the habitat is altered when people remove certain preferred trees. New species may take over, but the quality of the woodland suffers. Often a ring of bare land many miles wide marks the edge of cities and other urban areas because people (especially whose businesses supply fuel) travel farther and farther to find wood to convert into charcoal to sell.

WHAT WOULD YOU DO?

You Are in Charge
You are a politician in an African country with large areas of rain forest still standing. You are under pressure from a large multinational company that wants to grow palm oil in a primary forest area. Which of the following courses of action do you take?

- Agree to the plan, but say you will charge them ten times what they are offering for the use of the land.
- Resist the offer and explore the possibility of leasing land that has already been cleared of rain forest.

CHAPTER 3

Timber!

It is 2020, and Enriqué is a government timber inspector for a rain-forest country. His job is to monitor the government's sustainable timber program and ensure that all logs taken from his area come from rain forests that are properly managed and certified. The job is not going well, however. He knows that illegal logging is still common, even on government-owned land, but it is hard to prove. Enriqué has few resources to police the 2.47 million acres (1 million ha) he is responsible for, and he is not even sure he can trust some of his own staff. Recently, his family was threatened with kidnapping if he didn't overlook some illegal cutting going on in a remote area of his region. He is determined to do his job, but the temptation to look the other way is growing.

Tree Cutting in Progress

About 14.8 million acres (6 million ha) of rain forest are logged annually in the tropics; that comes to 23,000 square miles (60,000 sq km)—an area about the size of West Virginia. In 2006, the amount of logging in Southeast Asia and Central and South America increased, while in Africa, it remained the same.

In most cases, clear-cutting—removing all the trees—does not take place, at least not at first. Usually large, prime trees, such as mahogany and kapok, are chosen and cut down. Sometimes as few as two or three trees per acre are cut. However, smaller trees are often damaged—uprooted and crushed by the falling giant. Little is done to replace the trees or to allow natural regeneration. In Southeast Asia, more trees are cut per acre than in Central and South America or Africa, and clear-cutting is common. Poorly

DELIBERATE IGNORANCE

Illegal logging still occurs even where governments attempt to regulate and control the logging companies. Some governments even deliberately ignore these activities either because officials take bribes from the logging companies and do not report unlicensed logging, or because the officials lack the resources to police the area effectively. It is estimated that illegal logging costs developing governments about $10 billion in lost revenues annually because the income goes to the illegal operators and not the country itself. The worst examples occur in the Amazon, Congo Basin, and Indonesia.

designed logging roads damage rivers and streams, changing natural drainage paths and causing soil erosion. Meanwhile, the intrusion of giant pieces of machinery changes the forest ecosystem by frightening away birds and large mammals such as deer and jaguar.

Degradation to Destruction

Although the logging itself may only damage the rain forest, not destroy it, logging is only the beginning of the story. When the logging is finished, the farmers, agribusinesses, ranchers, and fuelwood collectors move in to clear the land for other uses. The logging roads act as highways into the previously inaccessible forests, opening them up to further exploitation. In this way, the process of destruction is completed—logging is the key to that destruction.

Making Concessions

Logging itself can be a legitimate way for a country to obtain income from its natural resources. Governments often grant what are known as concessions (logging agreements) to logging companies. These concessions are designed to regulate the number of trees that are cut down, but the concessions do not put a high enough value on the land. The areas of rain forest covered by the concessions are often in remote regions and, therefore, difficult to police. The agreements usually apply for less than ten years, which is far less time than it takes for the trees to be replaced and grow to full size, ready to be harvested. Without a long-term commitment, the company involved has no incentive to invest in proper forest management.

Only a few giant trees like this one may be removed, but many other smaller trees will be damaged as the big ones fall. Cutting the creepers and lianas (climbing plants that often bind rain-forest trees together) between the trees can prevent large specimens from dragging others with them as they fall.

Planting Trees: Good Idea, Bad Idea?

There are more than 148 million acres (60 million ha) of tree plantations in developing countries. It seems to make sense to grow and farm trees like any other crop, but the reality is often rather different. In parts of Brazil and Southeast Asia, for example, large tracts of natural or primary forest have been cut down in order to plant faster growing, more easily managed varieties, such as eucalyptus and acacia trees. Unlike natural forests, these single-species plantations are easily attacked by insect pests, and they often draw off so many nutrients from the soil that they deplete it, making it less fertile.

Some tree plantations can be beneficial, however. In Indonesia, for example, tree farmers replant large areas cleared by logging

Controversial highways, such as this road through a cleared palm plantation near Mirador, Brazil, increases access to rain forests. When forests are divided into smaller pieces, their biodiversity decreases because animals are reluctant to cross the highways.

AREA OF TREE PLANTATION IN TROPICAL COUNTRIES

Region	Area of Tree Plantation square miles (sq km)	% Total Forest Cover
Africa	30,800 (80,000)	4
Southeast Asia	448,000 (1,160,000)	62
Oceania	11,600 (30,000)	2
South America	38,600 (100,000)	6

Source: Forestry and Agriculture Organization (FAO/UN)

with quick-growing forests that can provide a source of fiber for paper and wood that might otherwise come from natural forests. Rapidly growing forests are also a good way of locking up CO_2 from the atmosphere, a process known as carbon sequestration. In this way, tree plantations can be an important way of combating global warming. However, in the countries where most deforestation is occuring, plantation forests make up for less than 10 percent of the amount of natural forest lost.

Trouble Down the Mine

Another cause of rain-forest destruction is mining. Large mines, such as the Copperbelt mine in Zambia, once consumed large quantities of natural woodlands to supply fuel for smelting (removing the ore from rock by heating it). Now, plantation trees feed such mines. Using explosive devices for oil exploration, as they do in Ecuador, also destroys forests locally. At the same time, the dynamiting clears the way for colonization by small or poor farmers. New roads, such as the Trans-Amazonian Highway, open up previously inaccessible forest to colonization and cattle ranchers. Secondary roads soon follow main roads, creating even better access. The roads add commercial value to land, encouraging land buying and more deforestation.

WHAT WOULD YOU DO?

You Are in Charge
You are speaking on behalf of an independent investigation that was set up to decide whether countries with large areas of rain forest have the right to exploit this natural resource (or the resources it contains, such as minerals) without interference from the outside world. Which of the following two courses of action will you recommend?

- We cannot control the actions of other states, even if we wanted to. They must be allowed to determine their own courses of action.
- The issues are far too important to allow individual governments to decide; global action is needed—and needed quickly.

CHAPTER 4

A Valuable Resource

It is 2025, and the news in the Democratic Republic of Congo, in Central Africa, is that the world's last remaining wild gorilla, outside zoos and conservation areas, has died. The number of lowland gorillas had been dwindling for years because of habitat destruction, wars, and illegal hunting for so-called bush meat. For many years, the population was too small to keep itself going, and, despite reintroductions from captive gorillas, the decline continued. The few remaining gorillas spent their last years hounded by film crews and weakened by disease that resulted from contact with humans. Finally, only one wild gorilla remained, but he became ill and died on June 31, 2025.

Rain Forests: A Global Resource

Gorillas still live in many parts of Central Africa, such as the Democratic Republic of Congo and Equatorial Guinea, although they are under threat from many sides. Other apes, like the orangutan of Southeast Asia, are equally threatened. The health and number of these apes helps us assess the health of the rain forest. Their survival depends on the survival of the rain forests, and the survival of the rain forests is crucial to the future of Earth.

It is easy to see why rain forests are so important: 500 million people still live in and around rain forests, depending partly or entirely on them for food, fuelwood, or other resources. Forest trees and plants are a global source of medicinal drugs, foods, building materials, and many other products. They play a central role in regulating global weather patterns as well as influencing local rainfall. They prevent much of Earth's soil from literally slipping into the sea. Rain forests also store vast quantities of carbon, which they have removed from the atmosphere as carbon dioxide, while producing a significant amount of the world's oxygen and rainfall. We may only be beginning to realize the vital role that rain forests can play in helping combat global warming, so it is essential that we protect them.

BEATING DISEASE

In a Mexican rain forest, a species of wild corn has been found that is resistant to five of the world's seven most widespread corn viruses. It is now used to add resistance to corn crops worldwide. The rosy periwinkle plant from Madagascan forests provides a drug (vincristine) for treating leukemia (a type of cancer), and the bark of a species of African cherry is now an important factor in the treatment of prostate cancer. Rain-forest plants may also be a source of hope for future treatments of HIV/AIDS, Alzheimer's disease, and malaria, all of which kill and disable millions of people each year. Rain-forest animals are important, too: vampire bats have a compound in their saliva that helps to prevent blood clots, and skin secretions from the poison dart frog may be used as a painkiller.

Even in parks like this in Rwanda, local wars and gold and silver prospectors constantly threaten gorillas, monkeys, and other endangered species. When mines are running, the mining crews are frequently fed bush meat—local wild animals that are illegally hunted and killed wholesale in the mining areas.

Welcome to the Gene Pool

Most rain forests are very old. Some have hardly changed for tens of millions of years. The oldest rain forest in the world is Tama Negara, in Malaysia, estimated to be a staggering 130 million years old—70 million years older than the last of the dinosaurs! The rain forests contain more than 50 percent of all species of plants and animals on the planet and perhaps as much as 70 percent—which makes them the greatest living gene pool on Earth. It is this incredible variety or diversity of life, called biodiversity, that makes them so important.

Opposite: **Orangutans live solitary lives in the forests of Indonesia and Malaysia where their habitat is being destroyed. Baby orangutans are often taken from the wild to supply the trade in exotic pets; others become orphans when their parents are killed for bush meat.**

Going Tropical

Tropical rain forests can be split into moist forests and equatorial forests. Moist forests often grow in highlands, swathed in fog, mist, and cloud. Moist forests are generally found farther away from the equator and receive about 51 inches (130 centimeters) of rain each year. They have a cooler, drier season, and the Sun's rays reach the forest floor when trees shed their leaves. Moist forests often have a well-developed understory between the canopy and the ground cover that is not found in equatorial forest. Moist forests are found in parts of South America, northern Australia, the Caribbean, West Africa, and Southeast Asia, primarily in Thailand, Burma, Vietnam, and Sri Lanka.

Equatorial forests are found nearer the equator. They receive more than 79 inches (200 cm) of rain, spread evenly throughout the year. They have the greatest biodiversity. Because of the lack of distinct seasons, the trees never lose all their leaves, and little sunlight penetrates to the bare forest floor. These forests—found in Papua New Guinea, Malaysia, Indonesia, the great Amazon Basin in South America, and the Congo Basin in Africa—make up about two-thirds of the world's tropical rain forests.

RAIN-FOREST BIODIVERSITY FACT FILE

- Rain forests cover less than 2 percent of Earth's surface (including the oceans) but support more than 50 percent of all known life on the planet. They could contain up to 50 million species; many have yet to be named or even discovered.

- A tropical rain forest may have 210 different species of tree in a single acre (.4 ha). A temperate forest in Europe or the United States will be dominated by only six or so species and will contain fifteen to twenty overall.

- Some trees can only be pollinated by a single type of insect, which is also dependent on the tree. If one dies, the other cannot survive.

- Where large-scale, rain-forest destruction takes place, tropical rain forests die one hundred times faster than they would naturally.

Separate Floors for Separate Species

Rain forests are like multistory buildings with different conditions and living opportunities (called *niches*) available to different plants and animals at every level. These levels are one of the reasons for their biodiversity. The main layer is the canopy, a dense ceiling of leaves and branches that catches most of the sunlight and uses its energy to produce food (sugars) by photosynthesis. This layer, therefore, attracts the greatest number and variety of animals.

Above the canopy is the overstory, the tops of taller (or emergent) trees that break through the canopy and may grow another 100 feet (30 m). Below the canopy is the understory, which is a broken layer of smaller or juvenile trees and, below this, the shrub layer, which consists of shrubs and young trees that grow about 6 to 23 feet (2 to 7 m) high. The lowest layer is the forest floor.

Where Dead Plants Lie

The forest floor is often surprisingly open, due to the lack of light penetrating the canopy and lower layers. About 70 to 90 percent of life in the rain forest is found in the trees, but this does not mean that nothing is growing on the floor. A complex community of insects, fungi, and bacteria live there to ensure that the nutrient cycle is continued. The hot, humid conditions mean that fallen leaves and other dead material are completely decomposed

In this primary forest, the canopy is so dense that little or no light penetrates through to the forest floor. Consequently, very little grows there, and most of the life of the forest is concentrated in the upper reaches of the trees.

(broken down) and recycled back into plant material in a matter of days. Whole trees may disappear in weeks in this way.

The combination of strong sunlight, high rainfall, and rapid decomposition means that rain forests are highly productive places. When a forest tree falls, seedlings on the forest floor compete to fill the available space, growing at rates of 2 to 4 inches (5 to10 cm) a day, to out-compete each other. Perhaps surprisingly, however, nutrients are recycled so rapidly in rain forests that the soil itself is often quite thin and nutrient-poor, which is one of the factors that makes them vulnerable to destruction.

Past, Present, and Future

Although we cannot stop the use of rain forests completely because so many people rely on rain forests for their livelihoods, we can improve the way they are used and try to lessen the more damaging effects. In doing this, we must think long term and try to make our use of rain forests sustainable, which means we have to use their abundant resources in a way that does not damage them now or in the future.

WHAT WOULD YOU DO?

You Are in Charge
You are responsible for setting up a conservation program in a protected area of rain forest in Central Africa. You have to convince your donors that your ideas will safeguard wildlife *without* damaging local communities. Which argument do you support?

- It is important to concentrate on protecting key species, like gorillas, since they indicate the overall health of an ecosystem and generate sympathy and support from the public.
- You have to understand and manage the ecosystem as a whole, including the people who live there; this may mean that key species are still killed for food, even though this may be unpopular with supporters of the project.

CHAPTER 5

The Climate Shifts

It is 2020, and the following is an extract from an article written by the environment correspondent of the new international paper *Global News*: "I am standing in the middle of what was once a rain forest on the Malaysian peninsula. What strikes you most is not the heat (which is intense) but the fact that most of the trees are dead or dying. Chainsaws have not killed them this time. It is simply too hot for them to survive. What scientists have been predicting for the past twenty years is now a reality. We have not heeded the warnings to cut down on our use of fossil fuels such as oil and gas. Carbon dioxide emissions have hardly altered, despite agreements made back in the 1990s to make significant reductions. Now we can see one of the results— thousands of trees dying of heat stress."

The effects of global warming are not just higher temperatures but also changes in climate patterns across the world. Forests are especially sensitive to climate change, so by 2020, one-third of all remaining rain forests will be under threat from higher temperatures. Satellites may spot large barren areas across most of the tropics. Southeast Asia, in particular, may be prone to widespread forest fires.

The Weather Makers

Rain forests make weather because the canopy of each tree recycles more than 185 gallons (700 liters) of water back into the atmosphere every day—nearly 21,400 gallons (200,000 l) for every acre (hectare) of forest. Large rain forests contribute to the formation of rain clouds and can generate as much as 75 percent of their own rain. Forests also contribute to something called surface albedo. This means that they absorb more heat than bare soil. When the rain forests vanish, more of Earth's surface reflects the Sun's heat, causing a warming effect. This, in turn, affects global weather by altering wind and ocean currents. Global weather patterns may become more unstable and extreme as a direct result of rain-forest destruction.

This rain-forest fire in Mexico may have been caused by the forest's reduction in size, which significantly decreased its local rainfall. Rain forests create their own weather, accounting for as much as three-quarters of their rainfall, so less forest means less rain—and more fires.

Warning Signs

Since the mid-1990s, rain forests all over the world have experienced periods of severe drought. In 1997, forests in South Asia burned for weeks as drought struck. Drought occurred again in 2005. This time, fires burned in the Amazon River Valley. Forest fires themselves further decrease rainfall because smoke particles interfere with droplet formation in the clouds. Although the causes of droughts are still a matter of debate, many people believe that they are signs of global climate change and particularly the trend known as global warming.

AMPHIBIANS FEEL THE STRAIN

Amphibians, such as frogs, toads, and newts, are especially sensitive to temperature changes in the water. Their ponds may be drying out as a result of climate change. Amphibian populations are generally declining throughout the world. During the last twenty years in the Australian rain forest, for example, at least fourteen species of stream-dwelling frog have disappeared or declined by more than 90 percent. In Costa Rica, the brightly colored Monteverde golden toad has not been seen since 1989, following two years of unusually low rainfall.

The Carbon Trap

Rain forests play an important role in sequestering, or locking up, carbon dioxide (CO_2) in their vegetation during the process of photosynthesis. They may, therefore, be important in regulating the amount of CO_2 in Earth's atmosphere. Of course, plants also produce some CO_2, but overall, they take in more CO_2 than they generate. In general, newly growing or expanding forests act as carbon storerooms, trapping large amounts of CO_2 for the lifetime of a tree, until it decays or burns, which releases the CO_2. Reforesting 386,000 square miles (1 million sq km) of land would sequester more than 11 billion tons (10 billion tonnes) of CO_2 by 2050, the total amount of carbon dioxide that humans produce in a year. At any one time, forests contain nearly as much carbon (in the form of wood and vegetation) as is present in the entire atmosphere. They are second in importance only to the oceans in storing and recycling CO_2.

Burning Issues

What is certain is that when forests are burned, degraded, or cleared, sequestration is reversed, and large amounts of CO_2 are released into the atmosphere—along with other greenhouse gases, such as methane. The burning of forests discharges about 2.2 billion tons (2 billion tonnes) of CO_2 into the atmosphere each year, accounting for more than 20 percent of all human-made emissions. Clearing and burning forests, therefore, directly contributes to global warming and climate change.

The way of life of the people living in the Central African Republic rain forest has hardly changed in thousands of years. They carry a deep knowledge and understanding of the rain forest itself, which has been passed on through many generations.

Cause and Effect

Scientists cannot agree on what the future levels of CO_2 in the atmosphere might be. Most think that the increase in CO_2 will lead to a rise in temperature of several degrees across the world by 2020. This rise, in turn, will lead to changes in global weather patterns, such as increases in droughts, hurricanes, and changes in rainfall in many parts of the world. Sea levels are also likely to rise, increasing the risk of flooding to low-lying areas, such as the Maldives. The effect of such changes on rain forests is hard to predict. In the Amazon, temperatures are likely to rise, resulting in drier forests and a shift of savannah vegetation nearer the equator. Trees may simply die of heat stress. Drier soils will mean changes in the composition of the canopy, which will affect the species that live there. In Africa, regular seasonal rain patterns may be disrupted, again reducing overall rainfall in equatorial areas. If rain stops falling, large areas of forest will become arid scrubland. Low levels of rainfall in the center of West African countries are already being blamed on excessive clearing of coastal rain forests. Deforestation leads to declining rainfall; declining rainfall leads to deforestation. Global warming could lead to both.

WHAT WOULD YOU DO?

You Are in Charge

You are a climate change scientist speaking to world leaders at a UN meeting. The previous speaker, a popular biologist, has argued that the threats to rain forests of global warming are exaggerated and that species will adapt to the changing conditions.

Courses of action:
■ You agree that climate change is a cause for concern but argue that many more urgent threats to rain forests, such as land clearing and logging, need to be dealt with first.
■ You argue that rain-forest destruction and climate change are closely linked and that the two issues must be addressed together as a matter of priority.

CHAPTER 6

A Dwindling Race?

It is 2020. The following is an extract taken from a recording of Katunga, an elder of the Yekuana tribe in southern Venezuela, shortly before the tribe was attacked by gold miners. During the attack several members of the tribe, including Katunga, were killed. "There are few of us left now, and most of us are old. The young no longer want a life working in our forest gardens and hunting for bush meat. They think they can make a better life for themselves in the big city and do not want to listen to their elders. When we die, who will carry on our traditions and look after the forest? Even now, our land is attacked on all sides from those who would take its riches but not care for its future. We hear our brothers, the Kayapo and the Iban people, have gone. Only two nights ago, the gold hunters came while we were eating in the *maloca* (communal dwelling) and threatened us with guns and clubs. We are afraid they will return, and with our young men gone, who will protect us?"

A Way of Life

Five hundred million people live in or at the edge of the world's tropical rain forests. They depend on the forests for many necessities such as food, firewood, and water. Of these forest-dependent people, about 50 million are native or indigenous peoples who rely entirely on the forests for their way of life. They know the ways of the forest and do not overexploit it. They gather food from small garden plots, which are shifted every few years. They hunt and fish in ways that do not threaten the resource itself. The forest not only meets their immediate needs for food and shelter, it also forms part of their culture and tradition. You might say they live in the forest, but the forest also lives in them.

Now that way of life is changing because, as forests fall, indigenous people lose not just their homes but also their culture, their rituals, and even their history. Their vast store of knowledge about how rain forests work—the healing properties of its plants, forest cultivation methods, even the understanding of its ecology—will also be lost.

ESTIMATED INDIGENOUS POPULATION IN SOUTH AMERICAN COUNTRIES

Country	Number of Different Groups (Tribes or Ethnic Groups)	Estimated Population (2005)
Bolivia	31	171,000
Brazil	200	213,000
Colombia	52	70,000
Ecuador	6	95,000
Guyana	9	40,000
Peru	60	300,000
Suriname	5	7,500
Venezuela	16	387,000

Source: Rhett Butler 2005 (rain forests.mongabay.com)

A tribesperson plays a traditional instrument (a *sape*) at a world music festival in Borneo. Cultures like these may be lost if rain-forest destruction continues at the present rate.

Attack from All Sides

The decline of rain-forest tribes is not just a matter of removal of the forests. It is more complex than that. As loggers, gold prospectors, farmers, and other settlers opened up rain forests, the way of life of many of the indigenous people has been changed forever, even where they remain in their traditional areas. Many have fallen victim to new diseases such as pneumonia and TB, against which they had no protection. Others have been harassed or even killed by ranchers who

Images like this, of a rain-forest Amerindian making the most of new business opportunities, show how rain forest people can adapt to a changing world. If this change is to be successful, it is important that traditional rain-forest cultures and values are preserved within a more modern setting.

wanted their land. Some have drifted from the forests to find work in cities or in government-backed agricultural programs, but their different background and culture has made it hard for them to integrate into these new societies. Often they have been shunned and treated like outcasts. The result has often been alcoholism or other social problems, such as addiction to gambling. Many have tried to return to life in the forest, but their lives have changed so much that they are now caught between two cultures. Also, it is often the case that the forest they once lived in no longer exists.

A TRAGIC END BUT A NEW BEGINNING?

In 2005, the tragic murder of an American nun, Dorothy Stang, highlighted many of the issues that confront indigenous people. The elderly nun worked to protect the rights and interests of small farmers and indigenous people in the Brazilian state of Pará. She was killed by two men, allegedly working for a local cattle rancher who resented her support for local farmers. Her assassination led the Brazilian President, Luiz da Silva, to send two thousand troops to the area to safeguard local forests and their people.

A Changing Culture

Outside influences have also changed the culture of the rain-forest people. Indeed, many indigenous people are happy to take on the trappings of the outside society. Modern dress, such as T-shirts and sunglasses, are now ordinary clothes for rain-forest people, particularly in the Amazon Basin. They often prefer modern metal cooking utensils to traditional earthenware. Many now have outboard motors to power their canoes and dugouts.

This attitude is to be expected, even welcomed. The forest way of life is tough and sometimes brutal. It is easy to glamorize a forest existence, when the reality is often very different. For example, local wars may break out between neighboring tribes, and life expectancy is often short.

A Clash of Ideas

Recently, many tribes have entered into deals with big companies that are eager to exploit their land for logging or mining. Sometimes both groups can benefit, but more often, the indigenous people lose out. For example, in Papua New Guinea, Bahineimo tribespeople sold off their land to a logging company, but it later emerged that many of the signatures on the agreement had been forged. Sometimes high-ranking tribal members, or elders, are influenced or even tricked into persuading their people to part with land. Occasionally, a clash occurs between the older members of a tribe who want to keep things as they are and the younger members who want to see the development of their land for logging or plantations. Some governments encourage these developments because they see it as economically good for the country; a few still refuse to even recognize that their indigenous peoples have rights to the land.

A New Way Forward?

The picture is not totally bleak, however. Partly because of international pressure, indigenous people in many countries are beginning to recognize their rights. Instead of being encouraged to

WHAT WOULD YOU DO?

You are an adviser to the Brazilian government during its efforts to preserve its indigenous people, while still allowing exploitation of its rain forests. Here are two possible courses of action:

■ The government acknowledges the importance and value of preserving rain-forest people's traditional way of life and recognizes that the only way of doing so is to create more reserves and protected areas, using force, if necessary, to protect them.
■ The government accepts that it is unrealistic for rain-forest tribes to go on living in traditional ways; it must invest in their integration into modern society through education and much greater financial help in such a way that their essential culture and character is not lost.

A coffee farmer in Nicaragua checks the quality of his coffee cherries (the berry surrounding the bean). Rain forests can be a continued source of income for local people by creating business opportunities based on natural forest resources, such as coffee trees.

migrate to the cities or onto agricultural land, some rain-forest people get help to continue living in a traditional way while also earning an income through paid work. This goal can be achieved by creating reserves on their original land and allowing small businesses and enterprises to run alongside a more traditional way of life. Not all indigenous people want this kind of existence, however.

In Brazil indigenous peoples have been recognized as having permanent legal rights to 11 percent of the land. Even so, while some better-known tribes, such as the Yanomami in northern Brazil and southern Venezuela, have absolute rights over 32,000 square miles (83,000 sq km) of protected reserve, few others have such full recognition. There are about one thousand rain-forest tribes, worldwide. We do not yet know if most, perhaps all, of these will gradually die out or be slowly absorbed into the outside world.

CHAPTER 7

Turning the Tide

It is 2045. An extract from an article written by the editor of the international newspaper *Global News* reads: "Twenty-five years ago, as a young reporter, I visited this rain forest in Malaysia and reported that it was dying. Today, it is a different story, not only here, but worldwide. Although the world lost many rain forests in the 2020s and early 2030s, the tide seems to have turned. Forested areas have increased in some countries, although it will take many years for the trees to become fully mature. Many species that were once close to extinction in the wild have been saved, including the lowland gorilla, which is now thriving in many central African countries, such as Chad. Many tropical countries like Chad, through a combination of international aid and their own efforts, have healthy and expanding forests. These countries provide resources for themselves and generate income from tourism and the export of forest products. The local forest tribes here combine many of their traditional ways of hunting and growing food with successful small enterprises, such as the branding and marketing of forest-based cosmetics and pharmaceuticals. Although it may still be too early to be sure, the world may have woken up just in time to save its most precious resource."

Statistics, Statistics . . .

One problem with monitoring rain-forest destruction is the reliance on statistics supplied by government, institutes, and other authorities. Discrepancies flourish. For example, in 2002, the Brazilian government announced that the rate of rain-forest destruction in the Amazon had fallen by 13 percent—only 6,095 square miles (15,787 sq km) had been destroyed by logging and forest fires, compared to 7,037 square miles (18,226 sq km) the previous year. The government claimed that the improvement was a result of increased monitoring of illegal activities and better land use. However, satellite images produced in 2003 by Brazil's National

Institute of Space Research suggested that almost 9,653 square miles (25,000 sq km) had been cleared. In both following years, the figures were about the same. It is hard to say which analysis was more accurate; they may both have been true because data often depend on exact definitions and meanings of *rain forest* and of *destruction*. The FAO (Food and Agriculture Organization), part of the United Nations, believes that destruction overall decreased slightly between 2000 and 2005 compared with the previous five years. Others, however, disagree.

Small Steps

Some countries have good news. Thailand has banned logging in its country since 1988. Costa Rica has now protected 26 percent of its country in national parks and reserves. In 2005, the Brazilian federal parliament passed a law on the management of government-owned forests, stating that forests are to be allocated for sustainable use, involving both private companies and local communities. Perhaps these are small signs that attitudes toward protecting the world's rain forests are beginning to change, and the issue is being taken more seriously.

A hiker crosses the Arenal Hanging Bridges in the rain forest near the Arenal Volcano in Costa Rica. Rain forests enrich all our lives, so we all have a responsibility to ensure that they continue to flourish.

TAKING ACTION

We cannot just close rain forests off and put a giant Keep Out sign on the fence. Rain forests are a resource, and they can benefit millions of people worldwide. Here are five ways in which we can do something:

- Establish more parks and reserves to protect important areas of rain forests and the wildlife that they contain.
- Restore damaged and cleared forests and plant trees, so that new forests do not have to be cut down.
- Help people live in ways that are less damaging to the environment. In particular, this means tackling poverty, especially in countries with rain forests.
- Encourage (and support) big business, such as the timber industry, to operate in ways that greatly reduce damage to the forests. Both governments and the industries themselves have to monitor and change forest practices so they are more sustainable.
- Be involved personally, and encourage others to be.

A Walk in the Park

Creating more parks and reserves, especially in areas with very high diversity or many rare species, is necessary. Already many exist, ranging from completely protected areas, where damaging operations such as logging and other activities are prohibited, to areas in which people both live and work. Success is more likely if the rain forest generates income for local communities by employing locals as guides or making handicrafts. Where this is not possible, the benefits must still be apparent. Allowing (and encouraging) the sustainable use of forest products is one example. Such activity would encourage local people to protect these areas by looking out for poachers or illegal logging. Currently, about 8 percent of the rain forests are protected to some extent, but many experts now believe this needs to be increased to at least 20 percent.

A SUCCESS STORY

Xingu Park was formed in 1991 as a means of safeguarding the Menkragnoti Kayapo people's land and culture. With help from international and other groups, an area almost as big as Connecticut, about 11,500 square miles (30,000 sq km), was established in the Amazon River Basin to allow them to continue and develop their way of life. Crucial to its success was a long-term plan to manage its borders effectively against logging companies, miners, cattle ranchers, and commercial fishermen. Now the community provides bilingual education and opportunities to develop income for its members. A satellite map of the area shows widespread deforestation around its borders but almost none within. However, conservation must ensure that continuous stretches of rain forest—not just isolated islands—are protected. Otherwise, they can degrade very quickly.

People of the Kayapo tribe at Xingu Park take part in a tribal dance in a protected area of their traditional lands. Generally, it is better to allow local people to continue to live and work in these areas. In this way, they are more likely to protect the areas themselves.

This fruit bat and birds like parrots are important in spreading rain-forest seeds and may, therefore, help to speed up the restoration of the cleared land.

LEAVING IT TO THE BIRDS AND THE BATS

Planting fast-growing fruit trees, such as figs, may attract parrots, macaws, and fruit bats back to deforested areas. It is hoped that the seeds from nearby areas in the animals' droppings will allow the gradual reintroduction of native species, such as figs and bananas. Even trees with larger seeds, like mahogany, can be spread by some pigeonlike birds. Both birds and bats are important pollinators. Their activity may eventually help to restore the area's biodiversity.

Restoring Land and Planting Trees

It takes hundreds, perhaps thousands, of years for a rain forest to become established. We cannot just bring them back, but we can make the best possible use of the areas already cleared or damaged. To do this we must increase the productivity of farms, cattle pasture, and plantations that exist on land that was once rain forest. For example, it is possible to grow higher-yielding crops or grasses that do well on degraded forest soils. What has become scrubland (land now covered in small trees and bushes) can be restored by tree planting and better management. Crucially, this will reduce the need to clear more forest.

Restoring ecosystems is most likely to succeed in regions where parts of the original forest still remain. Small clearings recover quickly by themselves, while larger areas need more careful reforestation (replanting). Secondary forests are much lower in biodiversity than natural or primary forest but will still encourage the return of some species of wildlife. Just as important, the newly forested areas can be used for the sustainable harvest of forest products, such as fruits and nuts, as well as timber. It is estimated that tree plantations of fast-growing species could meet the entire world's demand for pulpwood for paper on 3 percent of the world's already cleared forests. Meanwhile, planting slower-growing, indigenous shrub and tree species in other areas will help restore biodiversity over longer periods of time.

Cutting Carbon

Replanted forest will also absorb large amounts of CO_2 and sequester the carbon for the lifetime of the tree or longer. Doubling the rate of forest planting over the next thirty years would provide a carbon storehouse big enough to absorb one-eighth of current world CO_2 emissions, instead of releasing it into Earth's atmosphere. In Malaysia, there is a project to restore 61,700 acres (25,000 ha) of logged rain forest with tree species that are suited to grow on degraded land, together with species that will yield marketable forest fruits. Similar projects are taking place in Uganda and Ecuador.

WHAT WOULD YOU DO?

You Are in Charge
You are taking over the management of a rain-forest reserve. The previous manager banned any form of exploitation. This was unpopular with local people and expensive to police, but the forest remained largely unharmed. You favor a more inclusive approach in which people can benefit, too, but you are concerned that it will be difficult to control. Courses of action:

- You decide that the risks of allowing greater access to the reserve are too great and continue the present policy of exclusion. After all, you can always change it later!

- You decide to allow people to return slowly after talking to local leaders, even though there are risks, and some initial damage to the forest is inevitable.

CHAPTER 8

Value-Added Rain Forests

It is 2020. A rock concert to save the rain forests is being held in the new Olympic Stadium in Rio de Janeiro, Brazil. The lineup has been spectacular, and many messages of support have come from bands and politicians alike. Suddenly, a small, elderly figure appears on the stage. He is the chief of the local Kayapo people. He speaks to a silent crowd. "My friends, you may wonder what I have to say to you that has not already been said. In truth, I find it hard to know myself. I only know what my heart tells me. The forest is part of Earth. When we destroy it, part of Earth dies too. When we protect it, Earth breathes more easily. We can only protect Earth when we value it for itself and not simply for the things it can give us, such as land for our crops and cattle or for the timber or gold it gives us. It can give us these things but only if we let it live, let it grow, let it prosper. This is what I ask—not only for my people, but for the people of the world. The rain forest can be our future. This is my message to you all. Thank you."

Helping People to Help Themselves

Many people in rural areas live off the land, making use of whatever is available, whatever the cost—including the destruction of forests. Governments often find it difficult to balance their country's immediate needs against the longer term need to conserve their rain forests. One approach is to help the rural poor help themselves by improving and intensifying current ways of farming—a system known as agroforestry. This system includes growing a greater range of crops, creating access to new markets to sell them in while also improving the soil. This type of farming can exist alongside, or even within, natural forest, allowing trees and other woodland products to be harvested as well as crops and even livestock.

Without ownership of or title to a piece of land, poor farmers have little encouragement to maintain or improve the land on which they work. It is easier to move on and clear more forested land.

This Madagascan rain forest is part of a national forest program (NFP). Such programs bring together different interest groups and international agencies, achieving a more sustainable approach to rain forests.

Ownership is difficult to achieve for people with little or no money, however, which is why local (or micro) credit programs may be a good idea. These kinds of programs allow farmers to borrow money to acquire land and later use the facility to save their money. They also encourage a sense of business or entrepreneurship, and they can give people a greater sense of identity and dignity.

Tackling Big Business

Local agriculture focuses on growing indigenous fruits and vegetables within the rain forests. In contrast, large-scale agricultural businesses often require massive amounts of cleared rain-forest land and use pesticides and fertilizers that damage rain-forest ecosystems. By limiting or stopping the use of chemical pesticides and fertilizers, however, land and water pollution can be reduced. Using fewer pesticides would also improve the health of the laborers. Large-scale farms could use alternative natural methods of pest control instead. Strips of forest between plantations can act as corridors that connect sections of forest, allowing animals to move more freely between them and thus reducing the loss of biodiversity. These corridors also act as natural protection for plantations, reducing wind and storm damage, soil loss, and the spread of disease.

A STEP IN THE RIGHT DIRECTION

Many rain-forest countries are now adopting environmental plans to combat the harmful effects of deforestation. In 1996, Mexico announced its first national program to save the last remaining 10 percent of its forests. In 2006, Madagascar introduced a new plan to create protected areas that allow some resource use, such as limited removal of trees for timber to help reduce poverty. Small steps, such as removing the secrecy around bids for logging contracts and simplifying land ownership, may also go a long way to help rain-forest countries produce more successful long-range environmental plans.

Sustainable Logging: The Impossible Dream?

Can logging itself be sustainable? The idea is still a controversial one. Many ecologists believe it is impossible to take large trees from rain forests in a sustainable way because a mature tree can take up to one hundred years to grow. Few companies are prepared to wait that long for their next crop or to set aside large enough areas to let it happen naturally. To make tropical timber production sustainable, however, we may have to invest in the development of fast-growing, high-

Much of the damage caused by logging happens to other trees when prize specimens are removed. This innovative use of helicopters to remove felled trees reduces both the direct damage and the need for large access roads.

yielding timber plantations on land that has already been cleared of natural forest.

Where logging of natural forest does take place, companies need to ensure that removal of trees is carried out with minimum damage to the environment, such as airlifting trees. Ideally, trees should be replaced or allowed to regenerate naturally, which could be enforced through international and local laws. Tougher measures could be put in place to put a stop to the corruption of officials and the forging of documents claiming that timber has been produced sustainably. Financial incentives could be offered to countries that make sure this happens.

Everybody Counts

Most people are aware of rain-forest destruction but think they cannot do anything about it, which is untrue. We can all act to stop the destruction—both individually and as part of groups—no matter how small our actions may seem. These include supporting organizations that campaign for rain forests. Influencing those around us—our families for instance—in what they do is another way to help. For example, many food and cosmetic products are now developed from rain forest sources. These ensure that local farmers or indigenous people receive a guaranteed proportion of profits directly, rather than the tiny amounts allowed them by big companies who buy their products at low prices and then make large profits themselves. These products are often distinctively labelled or can be found through the Internet. When buying tropical wood products, it is essential to make sure the wood has come from a supplier that does not damage the rain forest. You can do this by looking for recognized, international labelling systems, such as the FSC (Forest Stewardship Council) program, which means that the wood you buy has come from properly managed forests.

A BETTER WAY OF DOING THINGS

Logging provides work for 100,000 people in Sarawak (part of Malaysia) and generates $1.5 billion annually in exports. Currently, only 1 percent of the area used for logging worldwide is managed and only 0.1 percent is managed sustainably. In the meantime, many developing countries are already getting more value from their timber by processing it before export. Turning raw lumber into sawn wood, such as planks, panels, and other wood products, makes it much more valuable. According to the International Tropical Timber Organization (ITTO), Africa now processes 80 percent of its logs itself, Asia 92 percent, and South America, nearly 100 percent. Higher value can relieve the pressure on rain forests by making those areas that are harvested even more profitable than they were.

A New Value?

The most important of the underlying factors that lead to rain-forest destruction are poverty and debt in the countries involved. Therefore, we need to find a way to increase the value of standing rain forests and reduce the value of rain forests that are cut to the ground. To be effective, these measures need to benefit the economy and well-being of the particular country.

At present, governments often offer people incentives such as tax breaks that encourage businesses and individuals to log or farm the rain forest. This gives people income over the short term. It also means they can claim they are developing their country's resources. Removing these incentives and changing development policies to ones that recognize the true, long-term value of rain forests would make destructive practices less attractive. This value would take into account, for example, the huge capacity of rain forests to prevent soil erosion or regulate water supply. One possibility is for rich countries to pay rain forest countries carbon credits that recognize the value of forests in combating global warming.

Many Measures

The rate of destruction might be slowed if the poor, small farmers who are the shifting cultivators are allowed space and protection from new settlers to continue their way of life. Loans and better training might also help. More efficient use of already cleared or damaged land could do the same. Better marketing of nonwood

Ecotourism is one way of ensuring that rain forests are more valuable to a country when standing. It is important, however, that such activity does not damage the environment and that local people benefit. Sensitive development and involvement of the local community can help to achieve this.

forest products, such as nuts, fruits, and especially pharmaceuticals, would also help. In Costa Rica, an agreement with an American pharmaceutical company means that a percentage of profits from successful rain-forest compounds goes to the conservation of forests. Increased ecotourism that does not damage the environment is another way of adding value to a standing—rather than a cleared—rain forest.

Facing up to Responsibilities

At the same time, the rich countries have to recognize that they have already benefited from almost unlimited access to the rain-forest resources of poorer countries—and now it is time to pay. One way of doing so may be to cancel much of the debt owed by poor countries to the rich nations and international banks.

None of these changes will occur easily or overnight. They will require cooperation between international and national agencies and governments and, most important, between governments and local communities. Only two things are certain, however: We are all involved, and none of us can afford to do nothing.

WHAT WOULD YOU DO?

You Are in Charge
You are a young person looking forward to a long and happy life. You understand that rain forests affect your future. It is hard to see, however, what you alone can do about rain forest destruction.

Courses of action:
- Leave it to others; people with much more power and influence than you can change things.

- Understand that you have power and influence too; what you say, what you do, who you vote for in future, all have an effect, even on issues that seem as big and difficult to resolve as rain-forest destruction.

What would you do?

Glossary

biodiversity The diversity or variety of plants and animals found in a particular habitat or area; a high biodiversity is often seen as a sign of a healthy ecosystem since it contains plenty of genetic variation

carbon sequestration The trapping of the carbon in carbon dioxide in plant material (leaves, stems, trunks, etc.) as a way of removing it from the atmosphere

concessions Permits granted by governments, normally to big companies, to exploit forests and other natural resources; the government gets useful income but often exerts too little control over the use or management of the resource

conservation The management of habitats or species to ensure their survival; conservation may therefore involve using or exploiting a resource (such as rain forest) to protect it

decomposition The breakdown of animal and plant remains by the action of small invertebrates, fungi, and bacteria

deforestation Removal of forest, usually through human activity; this may be because of logging, clearing for agriculture, fire, or other reasons

degradation Damage caused to forests by removing some, but not all, trees; often followed by more complete destruction as other users take over

developing countries Countries that are relatively poor and that rely mainly on agriculture and the exploitation of primary resources (timber, minerals, etc.) for their economy

development How a country or region develops, particularly economically; increasing industry may be one way; development can sometimes harm the environment but does not always need to do so (see sustainable development)

ecosystem All the interdependent factors, such as water, nutrients, vegetation, wildlife and so on, that make up a viable (working) habitat such as rain forest

ecotourism Tourism specifically aimed at allowing visitors to experience wildlife and natural habitats; this can be a very valuable source of income and jobs for local people but may damage the habitats themselves in the process

fallow (period) Time when cleared or farmed land is left uncultivated to allow nutrients to return naturally or by growing certain plants (e.g., plants of the pea family) that add nutrients through their roots

foreign debt Money owed by poorer countries to rich countries or banks; the reason for these loans may be to help their development; just paying back the interest on these loans can take up a large part of a poor country's annual earnings

indigenous Refers to any people (or plants and animals) that are the original (or native) inhabitants of an area; where it refers to people, the term is usually associated with well-established traditions and ways of life

niche A particular part of an ecosystem, such as the rain forest canopy, offering particular opportunities (for example, food or shelter) to certain kinds of animals or plants

nutrients Simple substances, such as nitrates and phosphates, made available to plants by the process of decomposition

primary forest Original or native forest, largely free from human activity and usually very diverse

regeneration The process of regrowth of an area's vegetation; it may occur naturally or be speeded up by planting trees

savannah Mixed grassland and trees found north and south of rain-forest areas and generally drier in climate; like rain forests, however, often a target for ranching and grazing

secondary forest Planted or naturally regenerated forest growing on cleared primary forest; secondary forest usually has a much lower biodiversity than primary forest but can still be

important both economically and ecologically

shifting cultivation A traditional form of agriculture in which land is cleared and farmed for a time before the farmers move on; the soil is allowed to recover naturally (also known as lying fallow) so that it can be farmed again

surface albedo The degree to which Earth's surface reflects or absorbs the Sun's energy; cutting down rain forests increases surface albedo, which means that more of the Sun's energy is reflected, altering weather patterns and ocean currents

sustainable Capable of being continued without change or damage; sustainable farming or logging would not harm the environment

tax breaks Reductions in tax; usually awarded to businesses, to encourage them to invest in development such as logging or agriculture

World Bank International institution that lends money to countries to enable them to develop their resources, such as minerals, water, and forests; often criticized for not insisting that proper analysis of the environmental impact of these projects is carried out

Further Information

Books

Bourne, Jo. *Go M.A.D! – Go Make A Difference: Over 500 Daily Ways to Save the Planet.* Think Publishing Ltd, 2003.

Parker, Edward. *Rain Forest People.* Hodder Wayland, 2002.

Pearce, Fred *Deep Jungle.* Eden Books, Transworld, 2005.

Platt, Richard. *The Vanishing Rain Forest.* Frances Lincoln Publishers, 2003.

Web Sites

www.forests.org
Forest Conservation Portal
Web site of the Rain Forest Information Center; acts as a gateway to other rain-forest sites.

www.mongabay.com
MongaBay.Com
Gives up-to-date information and statistics on all aspects of rain forests, much of it based on United Nations figures.

www.rainforestconcern.org
Rainforest Concern
Gives information about and campaigns for the saving of rain forests, particularly in Ecuador.

www.rainforestfoundation.org
Rain Forest Foundation
This site supports indigenous people and others who live in rain forests.

www.ran.org
Rain Forest Action Network
An organization that campaigns for the sustainable use of rain forests worldwide.

Publisher's note to educators and parents: Our editors have carefully reviewed these Web sites to ensure that they are suitable for children. Many Web sites change frequently, however, and we cannot guarantee that a site's future contents will continue to meet our high standards of quality and educational value. Be advised that children should be closely supervised whenever they access the Internet.

What Would You Do?

Page 7:
It is certainly true that this is a matter that affects your future, but this is not always the best way to get your point across. Arguing that this is a real-life issue that is highly relevant to your education (in all kinds of ways) may, therefore, be the best approach.

Page 13:
It may be tempting to try to maximize your income from the company by simply charging them more. This action will not address the real problem of deforestation, however. You might insist that the company invests in rain-forest conservation while still allowing them access to other land. You should be prepared to drive a much harder bargain that will ultimately benefit your people—and the rain forest—more.

Page 17:
It is true we cannot, or should not, control the actions of other states. However, richer countries are in a strong position to help and encourage rain-forest nations to save their forests in many ways. Examples of this include cancelling developing nations' debt, making beneficial trade agreements, and investing heavily in rain-forest conservation programs.

Page 23:
There is no easy answer to this question. It is true that a healthy gorilla population probably also indicates a healthy ecosystem. The best way to ensure this happens, however, might not be simply to protect gorillas. It may be better to concentrate on managing the area as a whole while ensuring the gorilla population overall is not endangered. Your supporters may not like it, and you will have to be prepared to explain the reasoning behind your approach.

Page 27:
It is unlikely that most species will be able to adapt quickly enough to avoid the effects of global warming. On the other hand, more immediate threats to rain forests (and therefore species), particularly land clearance, need attention. Ultimately, however, global warming may pose the greatest threat; it will also take the longest time to reverse. We should, therefore, address both issues now as a matter of great urgency.

Page 32:
Both approaches may be appropriate, depending on the particular area and tribes involved. In the end, however, change is inevitable and is often led by tribal people themselves. Tribal lands have been recognized and indigenous people have been encouraged in certain kinds of development, such as setting up small businesses and getting better health care and education.

Page 39:
You will have to make your own decision based on local circumstances. Whatever you decide, you will need to talk to local leaders and others before making a decision. What is certain is that you will need their cooperation, regardless of which plan of action you put into effect.

Page 45:
This one really is your decision. No one can force you to do anything. There are many calls on your time and energy, and rain forests may not be at the top of your list. It is worth remembering, however, you do have power—as a consumer, as a member of different groups (your school or clubs) and, quite soon, as a voter. How you use this influence is up to you, but many would argue, it should be used!

Index